THE BRIGHT RING OF TIME

David Clarke

THE BRIGHT RING
OF TIME

David Clarke

HIPPOPOTAMUS PRESS

ACKNOWLEDGEMENTS are due to the editors of the following magazines: *Acumen, Agenda, Envoi, The Frogmore Papers, Iota, Norwich Writers Circle Anthology 1994, Other Poetry, Outposts Poetry Quarterly, Pennine Platform, Poetry Monthly, Poetry Nottingham International, Ripley Poetry Association Anthology 1995, Seam, Smiths Knoll, Staple, Tears in the Fence, United Review.*

First published in 1998 by
HIPPOPOTAMUS PRESS
22, Whitewell Road,
Frome, Somerset, BA11 4EL

ISBN 0 904179 65 6

A catalogue record for this book is
available from the British Library

*Ten copies only have been numbered
and signed by the author*

Cover photograph of *Churchfields, Lymm* by Simon Clarke

Printed in Great Britain by
Latimer Trend & Company Ltd., Plymouth, Devon

In Loving Memory of My Wife

Susan

(1939–1996)

and for our children

Sarah, Deborah and Simon

If I could turn
Upon my finger the bright ring of time,
The now of then
I would bring back again.

On A Deserted Shore, Kathleen Raine

CONTENTS

THE WILLOW

Great willow
filling from far my window
I lie in my bedroom and see
you fur with green.
I have seen you stark
for long months, lifting
a huge V
from the dark
world of tubers and clay
to the thin snows.
I saw you let go
your leaves, as if they
had never been,
and stand
in a dead land
with frost drifting.

You looked dead,
but now sew
sleeves with green thread.
Perhaps when my slow
stitching to marl by worm
is done, from my rooted cell
I could confirm
my spirit lives
fresh in another fashion
to one who lies
troubled, where I once lay.
The sign you give
I'd give. Her intuition
would hear me tell
green-tongued tales from clay
and see love light my greening eyes.

April, 1996

11

CADMUS AND HARMONIA

It wasn't easy: all that pain
for no real reason—a daughter
melted by a thunderbolt,
a grandson torn by dogs, another
slaughtered by his frenzied mother.

Life wasn't easy, though they had
each other and the legend says
(after the vicious gods grew bored)
in exile and old age they were content.

In far Illyria they found
a warm and lonely paradise
of fern, pine, sunlit hills and lakes
and there, forgetting rank, lived out their days.

Transmogrified, they were at peace,
if peace it can be called, when life
consists of slithering through grasses
and brambles by the waterside
under the hissing sun to strike at voles.

MUNICH
(6 February, 1958)

The earth turns, spinning us through age,
light, dark, light, dark, to death at last;
a ball whose motion proved too fast
for that quick team. They left their images
in newspapers and photographs. The past
becomes a winter pilgrimage.

This day brings recurrence of pain
which endures, whirling like snow
through each year's icy reckoning.
My father's the last to board the plane,
its avenue of light now poised to know
the meaning of the runway's urgent beckoning.

Take off. The lives through which we move
at gathering speed must face a cold
crisis of understanding: what inspires
all we hope for, all that we love,
ends always in the snow's dark hold
on silence, broken fences, wreckage, fire.

An earlier version of this poem (calligraphy by Brian Sudlow) is
displayed in the Manchester United Museum at Old Trafford
football ground.

ANOTHER YEAR

Yellowed leaves blown down a gravel path
catch on old sacks near the barn, seek out old
shoes thrown in a ditch with boxes and tyres
and flap under flattened grass, the aftermath
of brutish coupling. A cold
October, the same as the one
last year, the same desires
consigned to oblivion.

Each year the change and fall of October leaves
herald darkening days, which find us prone
to the usual ailments and beset
by the growing fear that, somehow, all we achieve
is destruction of flesh and bone
and a collection of things:
furniture, books, letters, bills, the regret
the passing of time brings.

Not that this worries the chill evening air.
For a gale-force wind even men wrecked at sea
is just a matter of routine,
the howling of children, wives and their prayers
irrelevant, emotional debris
flung round the sun. Yet we still build spires
for the love of God, and artists are keen
to celebrate human desires.

At the end of the farm track the wind churns
the trees in a time that does not correspond
to a dancer's steps or the oldest clock. We know
kisses, etc. lead to the grave and we'll learn
soon enough what fate waits beyond
this cold October evening. Can we really depend
on a sense of the power of love and go
steadfastly on to the end?

THE LIGHTHOUSE

> "I have never heard him complain. I have never heard
> him deplore his ruined life or resent the treatment
> he had received at the hands of callous keepers."

Frederick Treves

That repulsive thing excited crowds.
It stank and muttered like an imbecile
decked out in tuberous tissue, shrouds
of skin, bosses of bone bigger than tangerines.

A creature to be sick at couldn't work,
know love or ownership, nor be held
responsible for his monstrosity.
The freak became a doctor's specimen,

hoping in vain there was a cure for this
abominable metamorphosis
which made him fear men's eyes and feel
a lighthouse was the place to live.

When, once, a woman kept her nerve, smiled
at him and shook his hand, he could not speak,
but slowly bent his heavy head and sobbed
to think that anyone could be so kind.

He died more than a hundred years ago,
but his courage and humility live on
in books, films, articles. The beacon shines
across a century's distressing seas.

AT CONISTON
(30, 31 October, 1995)

The trees burned yellow and brown, green,
golden and red down the road from Skelwith Bridge.
At Yew Tree Tarn we stopped
to watch the reeds and the light on the water.

Now, on this high terrace,
gently surprised we catch in the evening air
coal fumes from the houses below,
where friendly lights shine.

The mountains deepen. The forest
darkens and the town. As dark
seeps into the lake, bright stars
appear to sail across the sky,

as if to suggest we too must shape ourselves
for a journey. Ah, there's no shelter,
my love, from the night, though we return
to the cottage door and go in.

THE TOURIST

In monumental rain
he turned from Rome
and headed north—not like
those legions drilled to render
mountains into road—by rail,
knowing at the heart of things
corruption fructifies.

The city races round
a circus of trapped anger.
Another edifice enslaves
pilgrims in stupendous stone,
promising light. Bloody,
anchored in rite, both are on show,
their gods appeased by song.

What was he thinking, when the train
set out? What does anyone
who finds the destination is
a narrowing dark tunnel
and for whom the speeding whistle
of the past blasts its alarm
and shuts out singing?

GHOSTS

live in our garden. One stands
with a big giraffe, stares at the flash
and has vanished. One lounges against your skirt,
thumb in mouth, looks solemn and fades.
Look! There's another one in blue
with small fast legs, crashing
a tricycle on the ringing gate.
Racing a cat to sandpit
and slide, it disappears.

Other ghosts, too, wander the afternoon.
Wrinkled, not so steady, talking too much
but kind, coming out of the shadows of two world wars
to no greater peace of mind, there they are:
standing outside the gate and looking in.

April, 1994

AT CANTERBURY

When this place was raised, their hard brief lives
assured them of peace to come in the real, but
invisible world round the corner from almshouse
or mill. The market, harvest and carving
stone was their worship; not faith
so much as trade, acceptance of pestilent
raids in return for the promise of bliss.
God could be in the wood or next field.

Now old couples, widows, ruck-sacked
guttural young men, slant-eyed girls,
odd cyclists, children, lecturers crowd
round chalices, shields and effigies
of chain-mailed knights or follow
the wooden signs on a tour of irrelevant wealth
to a distant age of bowstrings, falcons.

In the melée with many more
a ticket of prayer has been pinned
on a pillar's notice board:

> *My friend*
> *Robert died aged 12 of cancer.*
> *Give him peace.   Laura.*

Near this pillar plague fires
danced, bells tolled, carts rattled
on rutted roads, few bridges
were safe. Her words
trade pain like a flail.

In the crypt's still place, in time's still place
of wish and question, there remains only prayer:
that Laura at Lammas-tide lacking shelter
and bread, and Robert taxed by harrow and reeve,
live still within soaring stone and stained light
these many hundreds of years from Becket's flame.

A VILLAGE GRAVE

A name, but no date or detail of what he did,
where, why; nor can his supine neighbours tell
out of the lidded ground his toil
on the farm or how he struggled
in a dull marriage, or if.
Talk of a lame horse, the weather, the future
must have gone on, but has vanished
like pipe smoke, like a smile.
An inn remains, cottages,
the medieval church. Was it a brave death?
Would death by accident add to his character?
Only a name, he's like the inner lives
the living lead, inexplicable.

The church clock's chimes suddenly end
casual speculation where the bank
dips to a racing stream. Thought
turns to the obvious, the only known:
locked in his body's chemistry,
into no choice eventually,
cellular instructions fashioned him
for calloused hands to put in the marred land
under now indecipherable stone.

TIME AND MOTION STUDY

Days pay the bills,
tell where work is, tick
for execution
as for egg and spoon.
Days turn to snow, then
daffodils. We live with that,

accept
this blue-white ball
never fails to spin
to Saturday, and feel
no need to brood
on what we'd do about it,
if it did.

PLANTING HERBS

Yes, he lived here for thirty years. His study's through there,
next to the dining room, where statesmen came to be entertained.
He'd show them the view of the parkland and offer cigars
and a girl or two. Even in those days, yes. Well, who knows?
Probably. You must see the lake. He created it,
you know, and have a look at the glorious herb garden. You
follow the path by the wall with wisteria to the gate,
then down through the wood. He'd sit by the water for hours,
thinking (I suspect) not so much of the eternal or fish
as of banks, the subjugation of bishops
and generals, and steel production. He liked music,
some poetry, painted a bit. A nation's fate in such hands!
Do take a leaflet. They're free. Hardly a film script though.
His first wife? Ah, she went insane and drowned herself.

She had a number of affairs. You didn't know? Oh, yes,
and he was extremely cruel: bound to be, I suppose, if
you think you're god and hate a woman who only gave birth
to girls. The servants didn't talk, of course, and the press
kept out of the way in those days, but everyone knew
of his uncontrollable rages and the effect
on his daughters was plain: one a psychopath, the other
a drunkard. She married an earl and died raving.

The second wife? She was interested in medieval things,
heraldry and the like. She planted the herb garden.
They were only married three years. Her portrait
hangs in the ballroom. When he died of some sort
of blood poisoning, she found it hard to manage
the estate. At any rate she spent his money.
On pleasure, mostly: you know, parties, travel. No,
she had had none of her own. Well, in her will she left the house
to her young brother, from whom the present owner is descended.
The guide book is three pounds fifty. The tea-rooms close at five.

TALLOW

After the passionate moan,
whether flowers or frosts prevail,
cells figured in flesh and bone
accumulate days
not of their choosing
on the journey to fire or soil.

From the sign at a water-filled stone
to a trembling song and slow steps
the now that is never again
moves to the light of real
lasting love, so we are told.

Yet children are hurried away
in the fangs of chance.
Do they sense the love exists
they never had time to know?

For others the waiting is long

but reaching the edge of the dark
like *ever and ever* in prayer
is compelling, hard, like
tallow that rolls down a candle stem
to be fixed by a sterile stare
after the passionate moan.

The song's out of fashion in these days
of obscene magazines and videos—
romance, an old sock, flung away.
On Lucy's wedding-day no
shepherds pipe, no zephyrs blow
lily and primrose. No woodland sprites are dancing
to a satyr's tambourine. Pan doesn't sing.

Still, this is Lucy's day. Intermittent rain
soaks the bowling-green in Hale
and shoppers, parking cars on the main
road, observe their own solemnities and trail
in search of Safeway trolleys. She can't fail
to make each wedding-guest adore her warm
smile and graceful form.

Since Pan is absent, all I can offer
is an ordinary prayer
that in this marriage her
love will be magical, rare
as a unicorn, and no demon dwell there.
Let her like mistletoe
cherish the oak where love grows.

With reverence may
her bridegroom bring her bliss-
ful gently home and say,
"So let us rest, sweet love, in hope of this."

THE PARROT'S TALE

A court in southern Sweden has ordered a burglar to pay £250 damages for shocking a parrot. The bird is now afraid to be alone and its owner has to drive it to relatives when he leaves his home.

The Daily Telegraph

I used to be happy on this perch,
lifting a claw or
bending a thoughtful beak
to clamp on a nut
and shuffle about a bit.
I'd ruffle a few green and red
feathers, awk, but life was sedate,
even tedious in winter with all
those Bergman repeats. Ah, Jim,
the ladder and mirror I liked
and the swing.

What spoiled it was when
that hairy barbarian
with a jemmy and big bag of swag
burst in and went, "Boo!"

Yes, I know I should be
more philosophical, awk,
regarding the shocks flesh is heir to,
but you were at work
and his clatter, bashing things in
and shouting, "Pieces of eight!"
has shattered my nerves.
For one thing, I can't stand the cat.
I'm not up to scratch.

You're not going out? Jim! Erk!
You heard what he threatened to do
when I told the police it was him!
I got you your silver spoons
and clock back, remember!
You can't just leave me like this!
Oh dear, oh dearie me!

I'll stay with Aunt Ingrid, then.
Or Long John? Oh funny, ho ho.
Just get in the Volvo, Jim,
and let's go.

YVETTE

At forty-three with thousands
to spend from the sale
of a family house he left
his wife to fend for herself,
packed in his clerical job
and set off, seeking
a dream anyone could tell him
was daft and did.

He lived well: two years in Paris
hotels till he found
the girl of those honeyed, sunny
days he'd treasured for twenty-five
years, but that didn't mean
she'd give up her husband and boys
because of her once golden hair.
They met a few times and talked.
When she made it plain
she didn't want to see him
again, with sullen words he went.

What he sought was not
what he got from then on: ill
health in a rented caravan,
his son estranged, the cancerous
death in a matter of months
of his wife. It was left
to ladies with meals
on wheels to look after him.

WHO'S WHO?

Identity is difficult to pin down,
as are what circumstances bring out the best
or worst in us, but would you agree torture
has each man's measure

more than certificates or bills, or birth, or
expeditions in wild uncharted waters?
Extremes aside, arms and legs look much the same
on every body,

so the clue to who's who should lie in the brain
and in time fastidious surgeons find what
gives men a talent for murder or breeding
pigeons. Can it be

just a matter of chemicals and neurons
that makes me a coward, you dashing and brave?
Like mathematics it's hard to understand.
Averages don't—

for instance—show your mind's garden, where you stroll
on warm days under cherry trees, enjoying
the benefit of immense wealth, or follow
the delicate path

to a shuddering encounter in a wood.
And statistics are useless in exposing
rapists and bores, *et cetera.* Who we are
certainly depends

on our actions, such as putting our fingers
in the till, and most of us know breaking wind
does not rate as high as composing a fugue,
though there are always

two sides to a question; but, if you prefer
the slaughter of war to something by Titian
and study the top-shelf magazines, you are
unlikely to read

or recall that Circe turned men into swine.
Perhaps who's who depends on whose side God's on
rather than all these genetic sequences.
Less knowable, too.

RETURNING, PAST LAWNS AND TREES

with a cooler mind
he sees two shadows bend
on the bowling-green's far side and fade
as the dark gathers over their talk
in the run-down colonnade.
What are they doing there
in the park's quiet air,
these summers all gone—

agreeing no use going on
and hopeless? Hardly. One,
pretending to study the moon, tastes tears
in that gloomy garden and promises
anything. The other steers
the biased wish from a hand
to a shadow that stands
on the far side of the green.

IN THE FAR NORTH

rocks rise like the moon. Down
dour glens water tumbles white
under cold skies and shadows
sweep over peat banks, boulders, bleak land.
Gaunt men here seem curt—no,
deeply consoled by lochs ringed with hills.
Fierce pride soaks the springing moss,
still shoulders the moving waters and air.

Kinlochbervie thrives and elsewhere
hotel breakfast rooms have still
not come to terms with cries
which never quite die away
from streams and cairns.
Thoughts of distant fires
flash on knife and fork,
on flint-lock, sword.

By the lit horn the land
plunges to Iceland. Saga,
almanac, demesne go down,
any need to return to the city
to reassert status
overwhelmed by water, lack of mercy, world.

ANTONY AND CLEOPATRA

He fought imperial campaigns
from the Alps to the desert, his shield
a world to shelter in, to take on gods;
and she—dark, smouldering with gold,
snaking her body like the Nile,
her smile a crescent moon.
Their urgent, shameless rutting
shook Rome's empire in the East.

Sad, then, to see them
in the coffee bar: he—bald
and snivelling, putting his glasses on
to read the bill; she—otiose
after adventures with a cream meringue.

THE SUBTLETIES OF THE GERUND

Gowned, posed, he stands among rows
of boys in a cheerless classroom
between the wars. Each boy
in his blazer looks bored, or braced
for a comment to make him smart
like the one nearest the camera.
A boy by the cabinet finds
it reflects his intended rank. There are
no girls in this public school.

The master, perhaps explaining
the occasions of the dative case
or the subtleties of the gerund
(useful to learn, this, when later
fighting a war meant hell for some of them)
is all too aware of the camera
and his stance shows his lack of interest in games
has been known for the thirty-two years
since he joined the staff with a first
from Oxford, of course. Furthermore,
his obituary may appear in *The Times*
and for these reasons he is important.

But so are the boys. Mansions and Ascot
are in their tradition and if they
are not involved in partitioning
Poland (just another example)
one day they may well be; so
one wonders by whom the lesson
in superiority is being learned.

FOR THE ALLIED WAR DEAD IN BURMA

Stone monuments, silence
and poppies raining red mean
nothing, if you don't care, or are
too young to know about railways,
maggots and the taste of rat.

Under the drumming memorandums
of high command (papers no longer
part of the story) men, named and addressed,
went to wear medals and headstones.

Soldiers who lie in that land
might have come home handless, blind,
brained by what was done out there.
But nothing was optional. They fell
to feed root, tendril, snout
nosing beneath screaming leaves. Shot,
starved, beaten to death, they would have preferred
other events in our vivacious cities
and notions of hills freely roamed.
Instead, their names are gathered on stone,
in poppies fluttering, in silence,
in somewhat inadequate prayers that seek
to reach beyond reason or love.

COCOON

let the world rage

my love moves quietly
as apple-blossom blown
by a small wind or words
unspoken like the touch of her name

let it rage

THE HOUSE AND THE DANCE

Turning, the lane leads
to a large country house behind oak trees
and limes. My feet crunch the drive
through tunnelled shade
past the leaning FOR SALE sign.

Dusty, mullioned windows
frown on the valley. The house front's
chipped sandstone gives up no fossils
of who lived here; an urn no clue,
tipped on the portico.

Did figures in black frock-coats half guess
days of dancing and wine would end like this
after a second world war
and shrivel to sepia? Here maids
carried their secrets down a winding stair,
a cook picked herbs, hoofs
clattered on cobbles, children played
with sticks and a dog. Now glass
lies smashed on the boards of a ground-floor room.
Ravens inspect the quiet decay.
The garden is wild. The agent
has gone away. No one answers the bell.

MATTERS OF COURSE

"...& poor Mrs. Wright what a breach death makes in our
acquaintance every time he pays a visit among them & what
an imperceptible impression such visits make with the world.
The newspapers are read by thousands & the Thousands of
deaths in them are passed over as matters of course but the
loss is only felt by the few..."

John Clare: *Letter to John Taylor*,
15 November, 1829

Watching bombs or rebellious cells on TV,
viewers can comment safely on things going wrong.
Remote, they feel in control. It's more disconcerting to be
there at woman's collapse, when she smashes the floor, scattering
the supermarket trolleys. Death turns chattering
customers away, is cordoned off, played down. And the day
carries on with the manager's apologies, pools news, birdsong,
but on this occasion there's no slow-motion replay.

And in the large, famous, imposing hospitals where fate
is properly catered for, lingers the odd refusal
by visitors scanning old magazines to contemplate
facts: that a loved one is coming to the end of choice,
that by degrees in deeper rooms off corridors a voice
hoarse, breathless, will be heard for the last
time. This has nothing to do with the perusal
of newspapers or sunshine and cannot be bypassed.

Even so, tall buses run past the hospital gates
every hour and take numbed relatives home through the sprawl
of shops and cinemas, offices, houses, parks, to the far-flung estates
where they'll sit with the *Get Well* cards. Later a priest may call.

NEAR JACKSON'S BOAT

I'm keeping the promise I made
many years ago as a child
to walk again from this sandstone weir
along the high bank which curves with the river-line
to the inn where the ferry once was.

A gate I don't remember, but follow the prints
of boots and bicycle tyres, skirting
the rowans and blackthorn sloes:
suburban scrubland, a dusty green waste.

Beyond the point where the water foams over stones
in a copse now dying and mossed I found him
hanged, still in the lunch time air, with a stare
and a grin which said he knew he'd be found.

One branch was torn off.
The great rending tear on the trunk
offered no reason, but gave him chance
to reflect. At the second attempt
stern wood and electric flex held.

Crossing a stile, I look back down the empty land.
Pylons stride over a greyness. The river
is silent here, where ivy, lichen,
nettles and bramble have achieved
their stealthy unchronicling.

The motorway roars on the river's far side.

The inn is still called *Jackson's Boat*, but the ferry was
replaced many years ago by a foot-bridge which connects
the Sale bank of the River Mersey with Chorlton meadows.

THE COMET

With us for weeks was this flare
coming from nowhere, from a time
beyond prophecy, beyond Thebes
or Aphrodite, beyond things
that once roamed the long-stone forests
or were spawned at the sea's dawn:
an object of wonder to watchers
in huddled gardens; to others
a mass of calculations, or
magical sign, a warning, strange.

If the great arm of God
hurled these sparkling icy stones
at the suns He created,
we cannot explain His motive.

Those who stand on our humbled dust
in thousands of years may smile
at our bafflement, when the comet
returns to prove their equations.

But who will read this and translate
its dead language? Let us return,
content, to the warmth of the house,
our marvellous death displayed in the cold night air.

ON A WINTRY SHORE

The sea collapses to lace and pushes a purled
irregular line where we stand, looking across the bay.
Further out strong waves collide
with an armoury of rocks and explode. The spray,
flung high and wide, subsides in the next blue-
green gathering swell, ceaselessly gripped and hurled
by millions of centuries of moon to
moan and slide.

But here, though blown and cold, we're safe to watch
storm-water and clouds, the last wolf or bear
long gone and no vile reptile stalking our lives;
safe but reminded, again, by the wind's tear-
ing shriek of our own kind's screams, which lunge
out of Russia or somewhere, and we catch
sight of creatures that hack and plunge
through the struggling air like gulls or knives.

THE NEW SECRETARY

I knew she was bright
when I watched her, three,
first answer the telephone.

She waited until its
dangerous ringing
stopped; then picked
the receiver up and said, "Hello."

*

A few years later I happened
to ask, "Do you know why
you see lightning flash
before you hear thunder?"

She paused for a moment;
then said, "Because my eyes
are in front of my ears."

LEAVING PISA

An immaculate place, the airport lounge,
until a modern Bacchus with a *Tango* can
totters into view and crashes on
a seat five yards away. He looks
like an old pirate, lion-maned,
and gives off fumes. His mouth
moves uncontrollably, as does disease.

Still, he's done well to get
past the airport patrol and assert
a dazed independence, however brief.
A change from hedges and starlight, too,
or under cardboard, where baths
or champagne are out of the question.

Our flight is called. I watch the drunken
tower lean and then, above the clouds,
I sip my gin and tonic, wonder
when/why things went wrong, and go on reading.
Yet, hell, he was some mother's son
at one time or other. I hate
to think of him pushed on his way—
a hostile descent to doorways and bins.

Then why did I pick up my small travel-bag
and retreat to another part of the airport lounge?

ANGLO-SAXON CHRONICLE

These annals' gutturals
tell how grim men
crossed by longboat over embossed water
to lay waste the land.

Savage with oath and sword, the heathen
host went out from winter quarters,
harried, burned, sent holy souls
to God's kingdom.

Famine came. Kings fought foes, killed kin,
took treasure, hostages. Battle-proud thanes
became beggars. Ruin was rife. Men
said openly that Christ and His saints slept.

Winds, rain, have long roamed wrecked
earthwork and abbey, where fire wrought havoc.
But cool, quiet rooms soothe the fury
on parchment, lock most of that misery in.

TO ONE IN PRISON

This cessation of liberty
shocks, the peremptory
apparatus of state
clamping down on the word *Guilty*
with reasons friends find no longer valid.

For you swam free, from a submerged
heroin cave, climbed clear of crime
two years ago, scaled its high
prison wall on your own. Menace
must be contained, but you
never offered it. Others,
tight-lipped, bent on aggression,
who can find no escape
from whatever has made them that,
are unfortunate, lost. But how lucky are you?

Shut in for no recent error,
believe—this is the legacy
of the past, its end. The future will
not be boredom, bad company,
this turning of keys in steel doors.
The future is your recovered mind,
your family, friends; in time
their outstretched arms, tears of joy.

A PLACE IN ROME
(Tuesday, 30 April, 1996)

It's taken a lifetime to get
to this tinkling bell by an ornate gate
in an old high wall. Inside
lilies adore the quiet, cypress trees lift
their dark fans, red camellias glow
and big white daisies blow
in terracotta bowls among the graves.
The rain makes the path's pebbles tap and shine.

Failing to free the mounted map's glass from persistent rain,
I walk up the slope, stop, read a few names
and follow the path to an oblong stone.
Here lies One Whose Name was writ in Water.

It's an acknowledgement of sorts
to stand here after so many years,
sheltered by a cheap umbrella.
Forty-odd years since I first read his Odes!
The rain begins to teem, violets
bounce and scatter. Rain streams down the stone.

He has become written words and gone
where words seek sometimes to reach: into silence,
with no discernible destination
except this wetted earth at the wall's corner
and admiration in a hundred cities.
He lies beyond moon-landings and Ezra Pound
and I belong for a time to the baffled roar
outside this grey wall and abandon
all notion of sense to the rain,
the battered grasses and green birdsong.

DAFFODILS

I wanted to keep
if I could,
a curl
at the nape of her neck
lovingly for ever,
light as a summer breeze
or blown as snowdrops are blown,

for its scent was sweetly sown
with most precious heart's-ease,
but death came to sever
its silken ring and wreck
the girl
who once stood
where daffodils leap.

MEETING PLACES

I saw him, once:
a shadow, silent
at a velvet-covered table;
I, four or five; he, faceless
with a mug of tea
in that dark room.

No voice or gesture; just
bowed shadow, dead in 1944
before I learned to count the days.

Last week at a whim
I went in search of his origins
and waited, in another room, for an event
to become a document,
for a name on a grave to be born.

A red certificate: my grandfather
(numbered in 1877) named
by William and Mary (formerly Park)
hiding behind their names.
But column 7 carries the shock:
"X the mark of Mary Clark, mother,
25 Dearden Street, Hulme."

That cross, more eloquent than a kiss,
lays her bare. What can be said,
except there's a likelihood the sun,
getting her out of bed, set fire
to whatever girlish dreams she may have had
and put her to drudge at a scrubbing-board,
which taught her to limit her own horizons?

UNDER THE VOLCANO

A small city is thronged
by mid-afternoon. Tourists
with cameras have come
in search of catastrophe
from places as far apart
as Melbourne and Manchester.

On leave from coaches and tea-rooms
they tramp the main streets, rutted
with chariot wheels, and visit
roofless houses, shops which had sliding doors,
the sauna baths, brothel, temple and square.
They take in the villas of the rich,
their courtyards and covered ways, note
pillars standing seemingly at random.

Some representatives of the dead are here.
One, lying back, grins as if he thought
it would never happen. Another
turns face down to protect her unborn child.
A third, with hands clasped over his mouth and nose
to keep out sulphurous fumes, sits
in the swirling dust. He, too,
can scarcely believe this barrage
of scorching pumice-stones.

Ten miles away the mountain,
arrogant in the afternoon heat,
made them wonder what god could
do this and why. Now, all around,
is clear blue sky. Beyond, blind planets whirl
and asteroids like furious stones.

SUTTON HOO

What went on
over this ground was din,
sweat and song, the ship
hauled up from the river and buried
below the man and his treasure.
Litanies, screams of men being killed
to keep him on course, steered the ship
to the land
and language of the dead.

Neither raiders nor ploughmen, we stand
somewhat abashed with our guide
over the long-gone ring-giver's gold.
On an unlikely Saturday afternoon
for ghosts to come flints glint
like battle-iron, the bitter wind
fighting off rain spears these mounds and rakes
that sparse flat land to the east,
where something is moving away. Over there.

AT WOODCOT HOUSE

I live in the place
where your spirit sings
in the light that brings
long evenings till late September
with drops of rain poised, as
our climbing rose leans through the air,
to plunge to the lawn, when you breathe—
or is it only the gentle wind?

THE BEREAVED

For three years at least
they've come to Judy's back door,
these squirrels, to pick up the nuts
she lobs on the patio flags,
where they crack and bounce.
Tree-rats, vermin!

Yesterday Minty the cat
mauled a small rag on the lawn,
chewed it and stalked off home. Later
the mother came, her tail a question mark,
first to the corpse, with a pounce
and sniffing; then Judy's door,
not for nuts, but to share
the knowledge of something terribly wrong.

Does a squirrel know prayer?
Gazing at Judy's face,
she sat for ten minutes mute
with raised hands; then scampered across the lawn
to hide in the oak. For nearly an hour
in the late summer air
over deserted gardens we heard her bark.

A pity that creatures such as ourselves,
despite our desire, could find no means
to assuage the grief in that wild calling.

DOVER BEACH

The sea is calm tonight. The moon
traces the incoming tide's pale lines of foam.
Long ago you watched a light gleam on the French coast,
heard the sea pound the naked shingle
and thought of Sophocles. So much has changed.

Other names spring to mind:
not the products of
an aristocratic lack of love
such as your age supplied,
and nothing to do with loss of faith
in the church; but names which have
shut your sorrows behind time's perimeter wire.
Our age started here, clanking, moving at night,
shuffling towards the snowbound commonplace sheds
at the end of the line.
And putting your arm round a girl
in order to face up to that
is no longer an option, Matthew,
for we can melt flesh in front of your eyes
in a flash that lit up the world.

The sea goes on grinding stones, slings
bodies up on the beach, will wash off
faeces, condoms, but never the names:
Auschwitz... Hiroshima... Auschwitz...
and after such knowledge what forgiveness
or future? Only strange comfort
in reaching the depths. None lower than this.

It is too fanciful to hear
in the ocean surge so many voices,
to trace in those grey wastes
their cries for justice, even sadness.
The sea knows neither right nor wrong,
but, punished by the moon, draws back
from our stained shores, turns stones to sand, endures
whatever spirit moves upon its waters.

SNOWMAN

He is used to wintering out
since the age of caves. Ignorant
of Xmas, he knew hardship
and fire, listened for mammoths and wolves,
watched children die in ravines beneath massive snows.

His mouth drawn into a comic grin,
his pebbled eyes staring, he now notes
a high-stepping cat's dressage
through garden snow, lets robins perch,
optimistically sports an old City scarf.

Thickened, blurred overnight,
he needs to be redefined: his boots
brushed, his civilised body flayed,
a dressing-down he takes for an ancient rite.

On longer days he leans
to the warm-windowed house for support.
When this fails, in mute rage
he sags, a wet sack, becomes
spilt freckles that slowly dissolve,
and leaves on the unscarfed lawn
two small stones: a Dracula bite.

THE CLINIC

The waiting room's unappetising square
fills, as stricken dodderers converge
from bungalows and neighbouring estates.
Checked in, they bring red plastic bags
containing files, which a dutiful nurse
stacks on the clinic desk to rise like heat.
Then, sitting on scuffed chairs, they stare
at the chipped paintwork, frosted glass,
cracked plaster or outdated magazines.
Tattered notices concerning
Crohn's disease and prostate health
flap, when an efficient doctor breezes down
the long grim corridor towards the desk.
Here auxiliaries sip tea,
occasionally call a name, the cue
for restless shuffling off, for lowered talk.

This is death's ante-room.
Are these drooling specimens aware
that the beginning of the end
is nigh? that having relatives in tow
to lend support or cause a row
will make no difference to a surgeon's skill
or cure the strong malfunctioning of flesh?
They seem dazed by it all, as if
they can't believe what's happening to them.
But it is, and it does—to everyone.
Sooner or later we enter the last room,
even if surgeons likc bees in summer
have paid the closest attention
to our clammy cells. Free at last
from TV dramas, the need to shop, drink,
some of these wrecks can concentrate
on what really matters, on what goes on
at the end of electron microscopes,
on the possibility of prayer, and of God.

IN TRANSIT

The tram rattles in to the city, stopping
where weeds, unhindered, sprout
between cracked flags
and figures, grimacing, get in, or out
to climb dirty stairs. Most
stay put. Doors swish shut with a guess
on the thinking of a shop-girl,
a bull-necked plumber and his sullen wife,
a brace of pensioners, three
ill-mannered boys and what seems to be
a bearded spy deep in a book.
Over the canal the tram winds past
the cross-stitch knitting of a cast
iron bridge and round a viaduct, its arches let
to dealers in scrap metal, cars,
wood, paint, old furniture. The homeless sleep
in heaps beside crisp cinder paths.

Changing to smooth, street-running mode,
the tram glides down from G-Mex
towards St. Peter's Square. Complex,
this whole, unromantic episode
with no real beginning or end;
an ineffable affair
impossible to comprehend:
the players unknown, the plot going nowhere.

MISTLETOE

It grows with luck on bare
apple boughs or oak, its roots
deep in gnarled rite, laughter,
chivalrous knight and horse.
The leaves in winter cause kissing.

Spellbound, it waits for a druid's moon
and gold knife, guards cradles
from fingers of witch and the dark, creaking.
At sunrise its bloodless berries
pulse like translucent wombs.

IN A GARDEN

Woman much missed, I will never say
our love's at an end, though you left on a lengthening day
and live now in my turbulent mind,
where I travel to find you
(equable, young, and kind
as you were and remain) who

had the most generous heart of any
one I have ever known. Many
a time, watching the birch tree's slow
yellowing, where we walked late in love,
I pray you are safe and approve
my search for providence in the fall of a sparrow.

Who am I to say whether your new
world, if it exists, makes you
happier, even in bliss? Such talk
troubles grief. Was your departing
indeed like this flower stalk
that rots in the ground to rise next Spring?

DICTUM: FOR AN EXPEDITION TO FIND A UNICORN

The going will be hard, pushing
through high forest ferns, with many days
on stony tracts in ice-cold air
below the snow line. Let the group
seek safe paths across escarpments,
waterfalls, rocks sprayed by mist,
where the white limbs of what they think
looks like a little horse might slide
or climb to drink at a hidden pool.
There must be gipsy encampments
to be visited and rough men
in remote villages
to shake their heads at the strange questions.
There are to be bears here and wings
fluttering in wooded valleys.
Disputes will arise and doubts
about the wisdom of going on
aired late at night round a fire.

Planning for this involves papers
for discussion and maps spread out
on oval tables. The chairman
shall explain, in a voice which is
clear and has authority,
the nature of the enterprise.
A civil servant will take notes.
Equipment, medical supplies,
the need for secrecy and the team's
departure date must be agreed.

Alternative scenarios
will bring this expedition
to its close. If these men believe
they've seen a unicorn (her neat
stepping with grace on tiny hooves,
her tilted head and horn acknowledging
this is a precious encounter)
there is to be humility
in their reaction to her long-
lashed beautiful blue eyes; no talk
of zoos; rather words of mercy
and adoration. If they can find
no trace of her smooth scent
and fabled magic and report
in a room with oval tables
there's no such thing, send them away
across the gravelled courtyard, each one
alone, under gathering clouds.

BEING CHANGED

They sway in floating weeds
and the shoal they sought,
their hair pulsing, framing dumbed faces;
or drift from blue-green to black,
from the bright swish of waves
to gradual dissolution, open-mouthed.

Hard graft with hard hands nourished them,
fishing the long nights, while their wives
lit lamps in ancient cottages
and, troubled by the gale's incessant roar,
wished they were somewhere else.

Where are those weather-beaten men
who only had time to think
of fish, the boat's planks and storm
that took them or the explosion?
Their atoms feed seas
from Cornwall to Iceland. There's no sign
of themselves but the washing sea
and wishes in the minds of women
gathered on the shore, pulling
their shawls close against the cold.

CIRCLES

These huge stones,
hewn and brought to stand
for the seasons' measurement
through skilled strengths
of ancient men,
hold earth's age locked in.

A megalithic ring,
pressing the moorland down,
they stand against grey sky.
Words of command
to guarantee sunrise
were given here as knives
turned to rumours running
to isolated settlements
down primitive tracks.

These stones are as strange
as the mystery of our own lives
wheeling to dark horizons
and a hope of sunrise.

A PARISH REGISTER

After three centuries
these lists and their death dates
impress. Supposedly,
out of a box of wool
sprang calamity, its cause
known then in the pulpit as sin.

Names that swell with summer's heat
taper to winter in Eyam's parish register.
Here is no stench of midden
or armpit, no screams, no clue
to who died how: in agony,
mad, alone. The people were ringed
by hostile hills, aristocracy,
rite. There was no way out
from these lists, this landscape,
except into legend and praise.

Yet the rector sending his children away
tells oddly against the tradition
if what came first was agreement
to stay. He was brave, but ambitious
until his wife's death taught him a lesson.

The villagers lived a regular round:
pottage, sour curd; slaves
to the lead mine, punishing winters, God.
When the affliction lifted, were those who remained
convinced of a power beyond their control
and, thankful as ever for small mercies,
keen to sing hymns going home?

ORPHEUS AND OTHERS

They come throughout the year
to stand beneath coloured glass, grief
dressed in flowers, holly and fern,
agonies masked by melody
and the peace of deep ground.

One once, it is said, entered an underworld
of spiralling, rooted echoes and mirthless laughter
to bring his love again to the warm trees
under a condition he could never meet,
when that other said he would let her go.
For, as the mossed path lifted
above the grey haze of standing pools,
he glimpsed a hint of Spring's first daffodils
and turned to celebrate in song.

HIGHGATE CEMETERY

On the western side a path
climbs past bracken and bushes, turns
its grass, leaves, broken bits of stone
beneath tall trees and aims
for higher ground above slabs, headstones,
epitaphs, shrouded in ivy, moss, convolvulus.
Angels lurch in deep green thickets, their eyes
fixed on the party passing by
with a confident guide. At the hill's crown:
some restoration of the catacombs;
nearby: sunken houses of the dead
surround a Lebanon cedar like a drum.

Fate, from accident to age, is hidden here,
fame, ill fortune, vegetation
gloriously intertwined. And we,
freshened by a light, autumnal wind,
find our existence verges on
the edge of platitude. So much life,
at variance from ours, thrives
in this burial ground: everywhere
paradox, resurrection.

AN AFFIRMATION

If I could snatch
light in my hand like thistle-down
floating to autumn soil, or catch
time tuning the red-berried air
and hold the note, the moment there,
would I be nearer knowing
what lit the dragonfly and is sowing
age in my face and hands?

Catch light? I cannot, nor know
into what darkness I must go.
Does every sojourner at prayer
kneeling alone
below sacred names
where sunlight illuminates the dust on stone
find only quietness remains,
that words are absorbed by air?

We are made to live here
with things that existed before they had names
against the days of meteoric rock and ice-age.
Above, the nuclear heavens rage.
What fashioned them
has fashioned us, a stratagem
which leaves us little choice but to make
something for our own sakes—
love: the mysterious best expression
of what we are
on this small planet, whose progression
seems otherwise arbitrary among indifferent stars.

DYMOCK, 1914

Here they gathered in days
the colour of gold to walk and talk
of poetry in untrenched fields
that final, innocent summer.

Many years later we came to this
August countryside in search
of the ghost of the only brother
Frost claimed he had.

Both summers now have faded to faintness,
as Thomas himself said memories,
everything would. And yet
a scene remains in my mind:

a ploughman with horses stumbling
along a furrow of charlock elsewhere in England,
where a man sits, conscious of war, on a fallen elm,
watching his life/time topple into the past.

CHALLENGER
(28 January, 1986)

Seven in single file, space-suited,
briskly step towards their time machine.
Neither they nor the newsreels know
the flight has been approved despite
some suspect seals. They prepare to feed
the nation's pride, to feel the stunning thrust
of the engines' computed precision roar them
beyond mountains, weather, everything known as home.

When it comes, the fire-burst down range,
an incinerating blast, the whole sky lit
and cracks blister the air like gunshots,
the trailed smoke thins into sunlight, wreckage
rains down, rains quietly down
on the raised voices of upturned faces,
while far above the elemental sea
fine ash is blown across the zodiac.

ELEGY

I thought, if I could draw my paines
Through Rimes vexation, I should them allay,
Griefe brought to numbers cannot be so fierce,
For, he tames it, that fetters it in verse.

The triple Foole, John Donne

ELEGY

1

She died on the last day
of the last year, when snow
came falling out of the fairy tale
and there was nowhere else to go.

These are the darkest
of all days
ever I have known.

Always I awaken
to the one thought:
Susan has died.

2

A still day.
Winter light
sweeps the lawn and hedges
and my slow fingers
seek to hold what lingers
of her spirit in the hushed house
and things she made bright:
her bed, bookcase, that green-
striped chair, a pen, these clothes.

Time has slowed, too:
rooms with her laughter
stilled, filled
with unanswerable silence,
an altered state of being.
I look through dulled
windows on a world
which daily passes by,
the garden gripped in frost,
the sun gone down.

And I am stilled, transmuted
into something I have never
been. "David,
I'm strange!" she cried
through her drugged suffering
three days before she died.

I am her residue of pain.

3

Rain has set in,
blurring the street's amber lamps.
I wonder what it is like
to have no earthly form,
to be transformed.

Say, rather, she
has taken fear
of death away
and in her going
left a longing.

4

Now she lies
with cornstalk and leaf
and I walk
unending avenues of grief.

Some say she is in God's care
and I cannot believe
such goodness as hers
does not still exist somewhere.

5

She did not die in this house,
but in a careful room
not far from here. I was there
when she went patiently away,
drifting like the perfume from a gift
of hyacinths, as snowflakes fell
past the window pane. She went home.

My kiss gave her release,
as if she waited
for a sign,
then sank to peace.

Now, unseen, I hope she is everywhere—
her hazel eyes, her elegant hands
and honey-coloured hair—
in this bedroom, on the attic stair,
crossing the lawn to stand
and gaze at the pond and the life there.

But she is utterly changed.
Does she now roam the orchard land
this house was built on
in an age of carriages and steam?
Does she know villein and reeve, Roman,
the primal forest and rock?

Her time is no longer mine,
but if I could see her again,
lifting her arms to love me again
or turning her face to be kissed,
I'd be content. If I could
hear her voice again—but she
is utterly different now:
different, silent, timeless as the light
that flickers through the willow's leaves
and makes them shine like tears.

January – July, 1997

73